SANDRA L. LASATER

45 Ways To Make $1000 Week/ Month

Make Money Online Or Offline

Copyright © 2022 by Sandra L. Lasater

All rights reserved. No part of this publication may be reproduced, stored or transmitted in any form or by any means, electronic, mechanical, photocopying, recording, scanning, or otherwise without written permission from the publisher. It is illegal to copy this book, post it to a website, or distribute it by any other means without permission.

Sandra L. Lasater asserts the moral right to be identified as the author of this work.

Sandra L. Lasater has no responsibility for the persistence or accuracy of URLs for external or third-party Internet Websites referred to in this publication and does not guarantee that any content on such Websites is, or will remain, accurate or appropriate.

Designations used by companies to distinguish their products are often claimed as trademarks. All brand names and product names used in this book and on its cover are trade names, service marks, trademarks and registered trademarks of their respective owners. The publishers and the book are not associated with any product or vendor mentioned in this book. None of the companies referenced within the book have endorsed the book.

First edition

This book was professionally typeset on Reedsy.
Find out more at reedsy.com

This book is dedicated to my friends and family who have always told me I can do anything I want even when I told them I wanted to do something crazy! (like learning to fly)
If you tell me I can't do something: I'll always try to do it anyways!

Contents

Foreword	1
1. Completing Cash Surveys	3
2. Organize A Garage Sale Online	5
3. Sell Your Expertise	7
4. Creating A Blog	9
5. Borrow Money To Make Money	10
6. Create An E-Book	12
7. Sell Your Items During A Garage Sale	14
8. Become A Fitness Mentor Or Activity Leader	15
9. Avoid Spending Money On Things You Don't Need	17
10. Share Your Abilities	19
11. Work As A Waiter Or Bartender	21
12. Rent Out Your Unneeded Items	22
13. Developing As A Freelancer	23
14. Create Websites For Others	25
15. Install Apps That Will Make You Money	27
16. Sell Your Photographs	29
17. Designing And Selling Designs	31
18. Create An Online Course	32
19. Sharing What You Know	33
20. Assist People With Simple Tasks	34
21. Advertise In Your Community	35
22. Volunteer As A Company Brand Ambassador	36
23. Make Deliveries	37

24. Having Fun In Town	38
25. Obtain Unclaimed Government Funds	39
26. Skip Your Vacation Time	40
27. Sell Items On Facebook Groups	41
28. Obtain A Loan	43
29. Visit A Casino	44
30. Make A Plasma Donation	45
31. Start Trading Forex	46
32. Establish A Dropshipping Business	47
33. Open A Credit Card, Checking, Or Savings Account	48
34. Domain Name Acquisition And Disposal	49
35. Pet Sitting (Or Walking)	50
36. Work As A Tour Guide	51
37. Purchase A Car Cover	52
38. Get A Part-Time Job	53
39. Get Paid To Exercise	54
40. Making Money From Your Parking Space	55
41. Work As An Extra In Television Or Film	56
42. Create A YouTube Channel	57
43. Market School Lesson Notes	58
44. Work As A Virtual Assistant For Someone	59
45. Set Up Households And Offices	60
Conclusion	61

Foreword

Hello and welcome to **45 Ways To Make A $1000 A Week/Month**! My name is Sandra L. Lasater and I am a 67 year young grandma that thought these ideas were scams. They aren't! If I can do it; so can you! This book will save you time by collecting the information so you have the resources all together to get started making money. With the internet taking up more of our time and providing supplementary sources of income, more people are looking for ways to earn money online or offline.

Some ideas will make smaller amounts of money but it all mounts up. Start with whichever idea seems easiest to you so as you succeed; your confidence will grow. You will make more money on some ideas than others but you must put in the time and work. Your effort is your only limit. **If you do nothing: then you will make nothing!**

" Insanity is doing the same thing over and over again but expecting different results!"

Original Author: Rita Mae Brown 1993 "Sudden Death"

(Although the quote is often mistakenly attributed to Albert Einstein - It wasn't until three decades after his death that he was credited with saying it: but Rita Mae Brown wrote it first)

1. Completing Cash Surveys

So please prepare to put some dollars in your pocket if you don't mind giving your opinions. Companies want to know what you think, and they're willing to pay for it. In reality, they will not only have to pay for your viewpoint, but they will be forced to. Around a decade ago, annoying survey agents would call your home phone around supper time and threaten you with a survey.

This attempt to steal people's time did not go well and really offended many to the point of taking firms to court for the calls. Businesses nowadays will have to pay you to find out what you think.

However, not everyone is aware that they will be paid to complete surveys, and even if they see an advertisement requesting them to complete a money survey, most people feel it is a fraud. Most companies pay for your time. And that is why, if you join up to be a survey taker, you WILL obtain a job and get money simply by telling people what you think.

You can earn roughly $10 an hour or more depending on how effortlessly you fill out surveys and how many firms you join up for. Some surveys are inexpensive (short and basic), while others are lengthier and can pay up to $75.

Here are some great websites for high-paying surveys where you may start generating money quickly:

- SpringBoard America
- Survey Addict
- InboxDollars
- Toluna
- Outpost of Opinion
- Swagbucks
- Pinecone Study
- Electronic polls
- FusionCash
- VIP Speaker
- MyPoints
- E-Rewards (I love this one! I earn Red Lobster gift cards every month)

2. Organize A Garage Sale Online

You don't have to wait for a spring Saturday to conduct a garage sale. It is possible to do it online.

In actuality, selling your items over the internet will earn you more money than selling them in person.

First and foremost, you must create an account on major online sales sites such as **Craigslist or Kijiji** (Canada), which is simple and free. Then, instead of displaying your wares on card tables on the lawn, you should shoot some beautiful photographs of them.

You'll upload these images for potential consumers to check out your merchandise so ensure you have decent lighting.

Hints:

- Photographed in natural light.
- If you need to film indoors while it's dark outdoors, you can utilize lighting equipment.
- If you don't have a lighting kit, place the object in front of a non-reflective whiteboard until shooting.

- After you've taken your photos, edit them to ensure the colors are accurate and anything extraneous is clipped away.
- Create an account on one of the previously mentioned websites.
- Create the advertising and upload your photos immediately.
- If you want to establish a price, you can do so or state that you will take the highest bid.

Press the Post button

- The website will send you an email to confirm the posting, and your online garage sale will begin. You can publish a lot of goods on one tab, or you can post a separate commercial for each item you have.

- The benefit of online garage sales is that you can get a lot of people interested in your stuff so you can figure out how much you can sell it for. That way, you won't have to accept the first bid that comes your way, and you'll be able to make more money.

- Be truthful about what you sell, and you'll soon find yourself selling a variety of items to returning consumers.

3. Sell Your Expertise

If it appears too good to be true, yet if you are great at anything, you can advise others on how to achieve the amazing thing. Most people now have a hobby or skill that they would not consider a career, such as cooking, gardening, woodworking, sewing, knitting, and auto mechanics, to name a few.

There are specialists who do all of these things, but they do not teach others how to do it on their own. If you're really good at what you do, you'll be able to monetize your gift.

Contact magazines or websites related to your craft or passion and offer to write an article or column for them.

It's fine if you have to do one for free because it will assist you in developing an online profile.

Join online communities, give advice, and let people meet you.

You can build up your website and provide advisory services or advertise in your local paper or on purchasing and selling websites.

People will approach you if you provide a quality service at a reasonable price, so get innovative with your own hidden ability.

Useful Websites:

- SmallbizAdvice
- Chegg (Formally StudentOfFortune)
- JustAnswer
- PollBuzzer

4. Creating A Blog

Choose a topic that interests you and blog about it.

If you choose a good niche issue and write about intriguing stuff, you can easily generate money with your blog.

The idea is to write about something that you are passionate about, so that it does not appear to be work for the blog, but rather a labor of love.

When you write about something you're passionate about, you'll be able to bring something new to the table, and people will want to hear about it.

When you have a lot of people visiting your website, you can put advertisements on it and voila—you're making money like nobody's business.

If you get the hang of it, you can even sell items such as books or other things on your website.

5. Borrow Money To Make Money

Borrowing money and having to pay it back with interest is technically a loss.

BUT, and there's a big, big but. Borrowing money to make money is a different story than borrowing money to get by.

Borrowing money to spend money is a slippery slope if you're happy handing away thousands of your hard-earned bucks.

Borrowing is a suitable option for you if the profit you make is more than the amount of money you have to pay back.

Of course, there are occasions when you simply must borrow money to pay for something that will not make you money—life happens.

However, if you find yourself in this scenario, it's a good idea to have at least a portion of the money you borrow made for you.

THOUGHT - *woot, woot*

If you borrow $1000, use $100 to buy things like wholesale key chains

5. BORROW MONEY TO MAKE MONEY

and resale them online for more than you paid for them, you will profit.

Borrow money as a personal loan and pay off high interest credit cards.

6. Create An E-Book

6. Create An E-Book

Writing a book is not as tough as it once was.

Nowadays, you can write a book about something you know a lot about and be confident that it will be published.

You don't have to rely on publishing houses to print and sell your books anymore. You can do anything yourself.

This is the age of self-publishing, which means that by taking control of all aspects of the publication process, you will become an accomplished author.

It's as easy as 1-2-3.

- You ought to write a book.
- You may publish an e-Book edition on Kindle.
- You can utilize Create Space to generate a hard copy clone.
- Your book will thereafter be marketed in the media.

6. CREATE AN E-BOOK

Amazon takes a percentage of the book price, which can range from 25% to 70%, depending on the program you choose.

Money is paid directly into your bank account each month. Of course, you can also publish a book on other sites, such as Nook Books.

7. Sell Your Items During A Garage Sale

There is no better method to get fast cash than to sell some of your old goods.

And the easiest approach to sell your items is to set up shop in front of your house. You can also combine with someone else's yard sale if you don't want to deal with the effort of creating your own ads. Friends or family may have a better location to have it.

- along main streets or roads
- closer to area activities
- more parking
- help with setting it up
- shelter in case it rains (rain or shine)
- put up lots of signs (cover out front and also major intersections near by

Additional collaborative garage sale!!! People adore huge garage sales. The bigger the garage's sales, the more customers will arrive. The more people there are, the more likely it is that you will be able to sell everything for a reasonable price.

8. Become A Fitness Mentor Or Activity Leader

- Getting in shape is a never-ending obsession for the majority of people.
- The long-term reason for this is that most people never get healthy because they start and finish programs almost like a routine.
- This also means that there are thousands of people in your city who are constantly attempting to be in shape.
- So, what does it have to do with you?
- If you can come up with an enjoyable approach to assist people lose weight, you can make a lot of money.
- Consider thinking beyond the box.
- Begin a hiking club and charge a fee for any planned hikes for individuals.
- If you know a specific kind of dance, start a class in your local community center, fitness club, or even your own backyard.
- If you know a martial art, start a class.
- If you are good at motivating people and are knowledgeable about exercise, you should consider becoming a personal coach.
- Create a bike community and arrange exciting routes to interesting destinations. You'll get some good workout while also assisting people in making new pals.

- Begin a secure cooking class.
- Pay a few people to provide them with a good new recipe every day.
- As you can see, there are various options, and you may certainly choose one of them.

9. Avoid Spending Money On Things You Don't Need

You may believe you require a morning latte, but in truth, a nice latte is more of a luxury than a necessity. Sure, you don't want to live in a world where you don't have to scrimp and save all the time, but you have to start somewhere.

Plus, if you discover that you can save a grand in a week, you may use that grand to earn more money, allowing you to have exquisite premium whipped, caramel, or chocolate coffee (If that is your desire).

Consider everything you spend money on during the week and then eliminate it if it isn't absolutely necessary, such as food, shelter, and transportation.

And they do so in the most cost-effective way imaginable, even when it comes to the fundamentals. Instead of eating out every day, pack your lunch and cook your own meal.

When you need to socialize, do it at someone's house where you can cook together and enjoy a bottle of wine. By the way, you are aware that restaurants make exorbitant food profits, such as 300%, so why not keep that profit in your own pocket?

Ask yourself if you really need an item or just want it ? Can I live without buying this?

10. Share Your Abilities

People are often very lonely, and if you can do anything to make them happy, my buddy, you can make some real money.

- Are you an excellent dancer?
- Should you juggle?
- Are you going to mime?
- Can you dress up like a clown and make others laugh?
- Can you still stand like a statue while blinking like a lunatic?
- Do you have the ability to sing a song?
- Do you know how to play an instrument?

If you can do one of those things, go out on the street and make the world happy.

Street performing can pay well if you're talented at what you do and honest and kind when you do it.

Know that even a dollar at a time in a busy place over the course of an hour will rapidly add up to $50.

If you multiply the amount of time you're out on the street by the number of hours, you might want to quit your day job.

11. Work As A Waiter Or Bartender

People who work in the food and beverage industries might make a lot of money, and they deserve it for what they have to put up with.

It's fairly easy to get a job as a waitress or bartender if you're a kind person who is eager to work.

Bartenders and servers in upscale establishments can earn hundreds of dollars in tips in a single evening.

These types of jobs are frequently filled through word-of-mouth at some of the best restaurants and pubs to see if they're hiring.

Of course, the base pay for bartenders and servers is nothing to write home about, but it's the tips that will have you sitting good at the end of the month. Just be caring and polite to all patrons and it will pay off.

12. Rent Out Your Unneeded Items

Is there anything you have that someone could borrow? Perhaps your buddies will borrow the items, but strangers may be able to rent them out. You can hire out items such as:

- Tools
- A musical instrument
- A bike
- Camping equipment
- Vacation home
- A room
- Furniture
- Lawnmower
- Automobiles
- Motorcycles or dirt bikes
- A snowblower- Just to mention a few…….

You can also publish your rentables on free buy, sell, and rent sites like Craigslist or Kijiji (Canada).

13. Developing As A Freelancer

- You have the freedom to do whatever you want with your time, so you can either optimize or waste it.

- If you want to make $1000 in a week, you should clearly not spend hours in front of a TV screen, but rather go to your computer screen and start working.

- You can begin right now, regardless of the time or day.

- You can freelance your time, and chances are there is at least one thing you're skilled at that others online will pay you to do from home.

- Writing blogs and articles is a typical approach to earn extra money if you are fluent in another language.

- However, this is not the only type of service you can provide.

- People are looking for virtual assistance with anything from website design to art, bookkeeping, and project management.

- Check out sites like Freelancer, Upwork, and Fiverr that connect service providers with people looking for virtual services.

- Most sites offer a free basic plan, and only a fraction of the money you earn is paid to you.

- Of course, there are update features that require payment, but you don't need to worry about that at first.

- If you have instances of similar projects, it will be rather straightforward to acquire your first freelancing employment.

- Don't worry, if you don't have prior experience, there are plenty of people eager to give newcomers a go for the correct fee.

- If you become a freelancer, you can comfortably earn $1000 per week.

UsefulSites:

- Freelancer.com
- Upwork
- Guru
- Fiverr

14. Create Websites For Others

You can, indeed, construct a website.

Me - What do you mean, build a website?

You may believe you lack the necessary technical skills, but guess what?

You don't need to be a tech expert to develop a website; there are several platforms available these days, such as WordPress, to accomplish so.

For your website design, you can utilize ready-made themes such as a full home page, banners, buttons, and other sections.

All you have to do is enter your information, including the name of the site and what it's about, and you're ready to go.

So, if it was that simple, why would anyone pay me to make one for them?

So, keep your expectations up there.

Yes, creating a website is simple enough for anyone, but not everyone has the time or motivation to do it.

You are providing a service, just like any other.

People can cook for themselves, but because they lack the time or ability to learn how to cook, they eat out.

All it takes is a few hours to become acquainted with the site you will be using before you can offer your services on internet marketplaces.

15. Install Apps That Will Make You Money

There are numerous money-making programs available, and while they will not make you wealthy overnight, the money you earn will build up over time.

This one is simple and just requires a few minutes of your time.

Download the software, enter your payment information, and follow the instructions.

You have just won a nice sum of money for yourself.

Among the things you can engage in to earn money through applications are the following:

- Participate in a game for InboxDollars
- Work as a secret shopper for Bestmark.
- Photograph for Foap
- User testing of websites
- Participate in Google Opinion polls

There are many more, but this is only a start. The pay scale varies according to the task's complexity.

16. Sell Your Photographs

Do you enjoy taking photographs? You will make a lot of money by selling your photographs. Don't worry if you don't have a fancy $5000 professional camera right now; you can still sell your images. There are companies that seek your "actual experiences," such as Foap, which allows people to shoot photos for various missions in their daily lives.

If you're good at what you do, you'll make hundreds of dollars. There are various internet stock agencies, such as Bigstockphoto.com, where you can enter and sell your images. Before you may sell on their pages, the stock agencies require you to send them test photos that they must accept.

You can also photograph local events and sell them to local publications. Of course, if you photograph anything significant, you may sell it to major news organizations such as Reuters or for a large sum of money.

Useful Websites:

- Big Stock Photo
- Shutter Stock
- Alamy

- Fotolia
- Veer

Make your own handmade crafts. If you appreciate creating whimsical, charming material, there will be a demand for it online. Often, customers want difficult-to-find gifts, sometimes they want monogrammed items, and sometimes they just want to buy work directly from the artists rather than from huge box stores.

Sites like Etsy assist you in creating an artist profile, after which you can publish photographs of your gorgeous items online. The nice thing about dedicated crafts sites like Etsy is that the users that browse the web are people who are looking for crafts, so you have potential buyers ready and eager for you to show off your crafty skills.

17. Designing And Selling Designs

Do you have the skill to design images, logos, or even wordy designs? If this is the case, you can establish a side business selling fabric, t-shirts, tote bags, and other goods with your designs on them. These design websites allow you to upload your unique designs while others order them for the thing they desire. You receive a part of the earnings from each sale. If your designs are effective, and clients continue to purchase them, you will be rewarded repeatedly!

Here are some locations to try:

- Cafepress
- Zazzle
- Teespring
- Spreadshirt
- Spoonflower

18. Create An Online Course

- People have a voracious desire for knowledge and skill, which is why online courses are big business these days.
- You can create a course on anything from "How to be more confident" to "Learn how to embroider like the pros for almost anything."
- If you have a strong solid understanding of how to complete your taxes, you can rapidly adapt it into a course.
- You can use video instructions, films, charts, and graphs in class, and you can have a lot of fun doing it.
- You can post your course to a variety of websites, including Udemy.

19. Sharing What You Know

So, how intelligent or knowledgeable are you?

- You might be exceptionally gifted in math or geography.
- Are you knowledgeable enough to teach something?

There are various locations dedicated to this purpose. You can mentor others online. In addition to school courses, you should teach your original language to individuals all around the world. And, owing to social media, communicating with people who want to learn English, for example, has never been easier.

- You may connect with people in Facebook groups and notify them via Twitter.
- You may rapidly set up online sessions with Skype or FaceTime until you interact with someone who wants to learn the language.
- Of course, you can still use services like tutorhunt.com, which are specifically designed for tutoring.

20. Assist People With Simple Tasks

Have you ever thought that having an assistant would be fantastic?

You don't have time to go to the dry cleaners, take your dog to the vet, or cook dinner. It would be quite convenient to have someone do such duties for you at those times. BUT you don't have the funds to hire a full-time helper.

Oh, no, that wouldn't be cool: but if you could only find people to do things for you when you really, really needed them. Well, you're not the only one that feels this way. There are a plethora of people who would gladly pay you to do these types of activities for them. **So, what's keeping you from becoming that person?**

Place an ad in the newspaper, at your local coffee shop, or online to let people know you can assist.

You can find someone to track you down and charge a fair amount of money for your services.

21. Advertise In Your Community

Your area is likely to be brimming with money-making chances that you have yet to take advantage of.

- To begin with, who doesn't require a lawn care service? Wouldn't the elderly appreciate someone down the street mowing their grass, raking their leaves, and tending to their flowers and plants?
- Consider what other services your neighbors might use if lawn care isn't your thing.
- Maybe pick up trash. If you have a pickup truck, you can pick up bulk goods or garbage bags in your neighborhood for a discount on days when regular trash collection is not available.
- As well as residences for painting. Power-washing decks Clean the engines. Take a walk with the dogs of your neighbors.
- There are nearly limitless ways to make money in your neighborhood.
- What you need to do is ask your neighbors for assistance with anything they require!

22. Volunteer As A Company Brand Ambassador

Ask local companies for promotional assistance if they want it!

- Yes, dealing with this one requires you to be somewhat direct, so you might want to start there if you have any solid ties with local businesses.
- You can offer to advertise the firm at local trade events or festivals, distribute flyers at grocery shops, or even undertake internet marketing for the company through blogging or social media shout-outs.
- You should try to discover some local business groups on Facebook and throw out feelers to see if there are any interested businesses.
- Make sure you tell them what you can give them to arouse their attention.
- Some companies will give you free products in exchange for a honest review

23. Make Deliveries

You can become a delivery person for businesses and individuals in your region, and you don't even have to be employed by a pizza company to do so.

Consider it similar to Uber driving, however you'll be delivering items such as meals rather than driving people to their locations! They also pick up items at the store for you.

Doordash is one site where you can sign up, create a profile, and start selling stuff.

- You will work using an app, where you will be able to identify available delivery duties.
- Toggle on the app whenever you are available to deliver and get paid immediately through your smartphone!

24. Having Fun In Town

Do you have any special abilities? Dancing, singing, and possibly playing an instrument?

- Why not put the money they have earned to good use?
- You'll certainly need to be comfortable in a crowd, and you should double-check the regulations in your area, but sidewalk entertainment might easily earn you $1000.
- You've always seen folks in movies playing their guitars or singing on the street with a money-collecting hat.
- Do everything by yourself! Offer your skills to your community and you will receive some donations on your own.

Who knows, for the right person, it can even lead to you being watched and given a gig at a local entertainment facility!

25. Obtain Unclaimed Government Funds

If you've never looked for money you owe but haven't claimed it yet, you could be losing out on some easy money.

- Go to Unclaimed.org and search for your state to find your Department of Commerce.
- Then part of your information can be filled out, and you can see if there is any unclaimed money.
- You could wind up with only $10 from a forgotten savings account, but you could end up with hundreds or thousands from an unknown trust fund.
- Anyway, it's worth a chance.

26. Skip Your Vacation Time

If you have a job that provides paid vacation time, ask your boss if you can obtain a bonus for working instead of taking a vacation or get paid for working besides your vacation pay.

You never know, some bosses may be completely fine with your suggestion just because they will not have to pay other employees overtime to compensate for your absence!

You might not receive $1,000 from it, but when combined with the other items on this list, even $100 or $200 will help you quickly get to $1000.

27. Sell Items On Facebook Groups

We have previously posted yard sales and yard sales on our website.

However, another approach to make quick money from stuff you no longer need is to buy and sell Facebook groups in your area!

Look for local groups on Facebook by searching in the Groups section for something like "[your city] buy and sell."

If you can't locate one for your location, try a county search.

You can add photographs of the products you sell along with their prices.

People can then comment on your photos to ask questions or express their interest. People are involved in arranging a meeting time and location through the private message.

Make sure you meet in a safe, well-lit public spot for everyone's safety, and tell consumers that you will only collect cash (or, if you have it, Square for credit/debit payments).

I strongly suggest cash due to scams and fraud.

Depending on what you sell, you can potentially make hundreds of dollars in a matter of days.

28. Obtain A Loan

People frequently believe that the lending process takes a long time.

- It could be, but there are now so many internet credit lenders that things are much easier than they used to be.
  - Look for an online loan that can be deposited into your bank account after income and identification verification.
  - Lending Club and Lending Tree are two solid places to start. They match you with several lenders based on the loan you require and your credit information.
  - Of course, you will have to repay the loan, so take this option only if you have an emergency and require cash immediately.
-

29. Visit A Casino

Caution ! Caution !

Of course, this is a hazardous tactic because you could still lose more money than you win at the casino. However, if you're lucky, you could walk away with $1,000 in your pocket.

However, if you are desperate for money and have never played casino games before, I advise you to avoid doing so. Leave this one to the seasoned Black Jack players who have faith in their abilities (and luck!).

30. Make A Plasma Donation

Although blood donations are normally free, you can donate plasma for a fee.

Important note: you will not make $1000 every week or even per month using this technique.

But I felt it was worth mentioning because you can donate plasma for roughly $100 per week or $400 per month, which can surely help you reach your goal faster.

Many donation centers may encourage you to donate up to twice a week for a total of $20 to $50, with a day or two in between.

The full process can take up to two hours, but it's not a bad pay rate for a couple of hours of your work.

If you donate frequently, you may save enough money each month to avoid requiring $1000 in an emergency!

31. Start Trading Forex

People are discovering how to make 1000 dollars rapidly by engaging in Forex trading. This technological style of trading is a means to benefit by selling currencies.

It's not usually something you can take up and start making money in an hour.

However, people who are dedicated about studying it will eventually make a lot of money just by trading in Forex.

It is entirely possible to make this your full-time job.

Forex trading, like any other form of money trading, may be dangerous, which means you can lose money just as quickly as you can make it.

32. Establish A Dropshipping Business

Dropshipping is a type of business in which you legitimately sell someone else's goods and order those products when they order from you for your clients.

Assume you run a clothing sales website. However, you can acquire all of those clothes from other shops where you can obtain warehouse prices.

- A $15 blouse that you buy can be sold on your platform for $28.
- If a buyer buys the shirt, they will pay you $28 plus tax, shipping, and other fees.
- The shirt is then purchased from the vendor for $15 plus tax and shipping.
- You make $13 profit and never have to store your own inventory or ship things!
- It's the ideal choice for a quick-start firm that can be profitable right away.

You have no inventory to invest in!

33. Open A Credit Card, Checking, Or Savings Account

Have you ever seen such incentives offered by banks to create a new account for a credit card, checking or savings account?

- Simply establishing a new account will usually net you $100 or more.
  - In some cases, you must complete a particular number of transactions or spend a certain amount of money before receiving the reward.
  - But if it's a card or account you're going to use anyhow, it shouldn't be too difficult.
  - Some savings accounts and company checking accounts can have bigger rewards, frequently worth $1,000 or more!
  - You may read more about obtaining these benefits on Nerdwallet.

34. Domain Name Acquisition And Disposal

Did you know you can buy domain names that you believe you should sell for a lot of money, then turn around and flip them for a profit?

- It is a real thing that people do to make quick money.
- In some cases, you don't even need to establish a website for the domain name.
- Simply wait for the suitable buyer to be located who is willing to pay for the domain name and watch your benefit materialize.

However, you can usually make more money with this strategy by creating a website for your domain, creating some vital content, and setting it up to produce money.

People are more likely to buy a site that they can visualize more than one that is just a name.

35. Pet Sitting (Or Walking)

Do you like dogs and cats?

- Why not care for them at their owners' homes?
- Pet sitting, like babysitting, is a legitimate job.
- When the owners are not there, pets can be loved at the home of the owners instead of dropping them off at the kennel.
- Many pet owners will be willing to spend a little more to have someone they trust monitor their dogs instead of kenneling them when they are away for business or on vacation.
- Don't you have time to look after someone's pets?
- What about walking the dogs?
- You can set an hourly charge for walking dogs in your community using apps like Rover and Wag! to take a walk.

36. Work As A Tour Guide

Are you completely knowledgeable about your city or town?

- You can become a local tour guide and show tourists around your favorite place while earning money.
- Sign up for Tours by Locals to get started.
- When travelers become available, you will be assigned to trips and must react within 24 hours.
- The company handles all publicity and behind-the-scenes tasks for you so that you may spend more time traveling and making money.
- You can also utilize Viator for something a little different.
- Viator pays you commission as a travel agent when you assist others in booking their flights, hotels, and vacations.

37. Purchase A Car Cover

Not what you think !

You could end up with several hundred dollars extra per month, and occasionally even $1,000 or more! Wrap your car in advertisements.

- It is determined by what you drive and how frequently you drive.
- If you commute vast distances to work every day or travel hundreds to thousands of miles every month, you will most likely do so by earning top pay.

Check out Wrapify, which is ideal for advertising that want to use your vehicle to provide chances for their business.

- You can also use Carvertise, which will provide you with more options.
- Even local companies with advertise with magnet signs on you automobile

38. Get A Part-Time Job

A part-time job in addition to your regular career may not be the best situation for you to generate additional money. However, if you're looking to save $1,000 every month, this could be one of the simplest methods to do so.

If you can find something that pays $15 an hour, you may only need to work up to 20 hours a week to earn enough to get your $1,000.

Of course, if you find something that pays better, you can earn more money in less time!

When you're in a bind, making the extra money you need temporarily may be the best answer. It doesn't have to be for a lifetime. Just work a 2nd job until you are caught up with your expenses or keep working for extra spending money for things you can't afford now.

39. Get Paid To Exercise

Do you enjoy exercising?

- Earn money while doing it!
- Yes, we all need to exercise to be healthy and fit, but it's even easier when you can get paid to do it.
- Sweatcoin is a walking app that pays you based on the distance you walk.
- You can turn in what you got to obtain prizes or cash.
- FitGift is an app for your phone where you can earn rewards from stores
- Both HealthyWage and DietBet allow you to wager on weight loss or join weight loss challenges and group bets to earn money based on the weight you drop.

40. Making Money From Your Parking Space

When you are not using it, start to rent out your parking place at work or at home, and you may wind up with the extra cash you require each month.

- After all, what good is an empty parking place if you're not using it?
- You might be able to find a site where parking your car is a little less handy and enjoy the benefits of renting out your space 24/7 to other individuals who require it.
- SpotHero will send you a monthly check or direct deposit transfer if you win anything.

41. Work As An Extra In Television Or Film

Do you reside in an area where TV shows and movies are frequently filmed? If so, you can try your luck as an extra on a set. Extras can make a good living, especially if they are needed for a few days or longer.

According to Backstage!, it's not uncommon to earn between $100 and $200 each day as an extra. Get a couple of those assignments every month and you'll easily earn some extra income. you might be surprised how many films are shot near you!

42. Create A YouTube Channel

42. Create A YouTube Channel

It is not always easy to grow a YouTube channel, but it is simple to start one.

- Even if you don't start making money right immediately, you can still create content and grow your channel in your spare time.
- Eventually, you will be fortunate enough on the platform to gain some recognition, which will easily provide you with the money you require each month and beyond!
- Build up your following and get sponsors to pay for your time reviewing their products
- Most of the time the items are donated to you. Win - Win !

43. Market School Lesson Notes

Selling college class notes is a legitimate thing that can help you generate additional money, but it will not pay all of your bills. Nonetheless, if you're a great note taker with a keen eye for detail, this could be a tremendous opportunity for you.

- Some places may allow you to put your notes on their website when they require them and will pay you a fee to sell them to others.
- Others may assign you to attend a class and take notes for anyone who needs your assistance.
- These businesses operate in different ways, but they all provide a simple method to generate money outside of a job.

44. Work As A Virtual Assistant For Someone

Digital aid is a wonderful way to profit from your skills.
There is no need to take online classes or obtain another degree to learn how to become a virtual assistant who assists people with assignments.

You can choose what you want to perform as a virtual assistant based on your skills, such as managing social media profiles, focusing on lead generation for organizations, or writing and editing blog entries.

There are various virtual assistant groups on Facebook that can help you locate customers, but you can also find virtual assistant employment on freelance sites like Upwork.

45. Set Up Households And Offices

Put your organizing skills to use by being paid to organize homes and businesses!

You can earn money in this sector by doing anything from building new storage facilities to teaching individuals how to properly file all of their documents or clear up their closets.

Take on a few clients each month, work a few hours for each one, and you may easily raise $1,000 or more by charging a professional fee of $30 an hour or more.

Some businesses hire people to set up houses for people that are being tranferred.

Conclusion

As we've seen, there are lots of ways to earn $1000 every week. So, take on this challenge and try as many items as you can to see what numbers you can come up with. Don't be too hard on yourself if you don't get showered in money the first week.

But once you start and you make money the first week, and the weeks after that, then go bigger and bigger. Spread your wings and fly!

Don't let anyone tell you that you can't do something!

www.ingramcontent.com/pod-product-compliance
Lightning Source LLC
Chambersburg PA
CBHW070316220526
45465CB00004B/1874